Dundee's Buses

London Calling

Derek Simpson

Contents

Front cover picture: Turning into the Seagate from St Andrew Street 225 (KGK 742) is unusually on the 19 from Kirkton as it makes its way to Shore Terrace. The roof seems to have had quite a thump from over-hanging branches.
Strathtay Scottish SR1 (WLT 943) sits at Ashludie Hospital in the watery autumn sunshine as it waits to make the trip that will see the bus cross the Tay Road Bridge to Wormit.

Rear cover picture: The Optare Excels spent a lot of time on the Dryburgh service as demonstrated by 205 (R408 HWU) pictured in the High Street whilst on the 2.

First Published 2024

ISBN : 978 -1-399995-44-8

Printed by The Amadeus Press, Cleckheaton, BD19 4TQ.

Acknowledgements

This book represents a departure for me in that for the first time I have included a bus operator other than Dundee Corporation or their successors. I would say at the outset that the book is not meant to be a history lesson on the RT or the Routemaster as this has been documented comprehensively many times before (far better than I could have). But I hope you enjoy this trip down memory lane right up to the present day. Although photographed Strathtay Scottish buses in the late 80s and early 90s my interest was a casual one. That said I always took the opportunity to travel on their Routemasters whenever I could; there was just something wonderfully nostalgic about them. I would like to place on record my thanks to Sholto Thomas (former Commercial Director with Strathtay Scottish) and to Graham Martin-Bates who have guided me through the Strathtay and A&C McLennan chapters. Their assistance has been invaluable and I consider myself fortunate to be able to call on their knowledge and photographs. I am also grateful to the many enthusiasts who have helped me during the course of pulling the book together: you know who you are, thank you. As ever unless otherwise stated the photographs are either taken by me or are part of my collection. Every effort is taken to identify and seek permission to use the photographs in the book. However if I have inadvertently used copyright material without permission or acknowledgement then I apologise and will make the necessary correction at the first opportunity. Lastly as ever huge thanks to my wife Heather for her unwavering support throughout the researching and writing of this book.

Introduction

To the less informed the connection between London and Dundee buses might not be immediately obvious. There is a clue in the title of the book 'Dundee's buses – London Calling'. Little did I realise when I started researching this book that there would be well over 160 buses over the last eighty or so years that have moved between the two cities either as permanent moves or as loans. The number of buses to make the journey really surprised me; it's funny how these things just creep up on you! The book's purpose is to show how this connection has endured since the dark days of the London Blitz in 1940 to the present day. The two main operating companies in the city, that is Dundee Corporation and Strathtay Scottish together with their successors, are the main focus with a little detour to A&C McLennan of Spittalfield who also operated a small number of ex-London Transport RTL's in the 60s and 70s on their Dundee-Errol service. I appreciate that both Fife Scottish and Moffat and Williamson have run the odd ex-London bus to Dundee but I have chosen to concentrate on those entities based north of the Tay so please forgive me for that. My previous books have gone into detail regarding Dundee Corporation's intake of ex-London Transport buses in the 1950s but as ever there is still a bit more to tell and hopefully I have avoided any duplication as far as possible without dumbing down the story too much. These early ex-London purchases would eventually be withdrawn in the late 60s when A&C McLennan buses would continue the London connection until the early 70s. For the next dozen or so years there was a bit of a lull aside from the odd transfer south, principally Dundee's first open top bus. In 1986, anyone who either lived in or visited Dundee could not have failed to notice the striking ex-London Routemasters running in the city. With their half cab, rear entrance design, eye catching livery and a conductor taking the fares they certainly caught the public's imagination. Such was the success of the conductors they outlasted the Routemasters right up until 2020 when Covid-19 pandemic social distancing rules and staff safety finally saw the service cease. The sight of these old stalwarts running around Dundee and the surrounding area was somewhat ironic given that eight younger Tayside Ailsas had made the journey south to work on London Transport tendered routes such were the vagaries of the industry at that time. Fast forward to the 21st Century, Strathtay would operate two 'New' Routemasters (the only ones to operate outside London) and send buses to help move people at the 2012 London Olympic Games. National Express Group (now the owners of Tayside Public Transport Co Ltd trading as Travel Dundee then National Express Dundee and ultimately Xplore Dundee) took the opportunity to send some of their low-floor ex-Travel London buses up to the City of Discovery to allow the fleet to become 100% low-floor. Last but by no means least bringing us up to date McGill's Bus Services the present owners of Xplore Dundee have brought a further thirteen ADL Enviro 400s and a selection of open-top buses from London to the city meaning that the connection today is just as strong as it ever was. Hopefully the extent of the transfers will become clear as you thumb through this book.

The old High Street is gradually being demolished behind the advertising hoardings as 222 (JXC 182) loads up for Fintry in this early 60s view.

A vehicle shortage has contributed to SR22 (AST 416A) working on service 51 to Fowlis and Liff villages. Heading up the Gourdie Brae must have been a challenge not to mention some of the narrow country roads in that neck of the woods. The bus was saved from the scrap yard and is now a mobile tearoom in London.

8980 (YX62 BFG) shows off the Xplore Dundee livery to good effect when spotted in November 2023

Dundee Corporation Transport and its successors

A call for help

Dundee Corporation Transport Fleet Number	Registration Number
35	TS 9117
36	TS 9118
38	TS 9120
40	TS 9122
44	TS 9124

Typical of the buses sent from Dundee to London during World War Two is 38 (TS 9120) seen in Dundee whilst running to Broughty Ferry. New in 1931 this was a Leyland TD1 with Leyland bodywork. This was one of the last Leyland buses bought by Dundee that moved to AEC and Daimlers in future years.

As ever the best place to start is the beginning which takes us back to the Second World War and in particular the London Blitz in 1940 which was stretching the city's transport infrastructure to breaking point. London Transport issued an appeal on the 17th October 1940 for buses due to the number of their vehicles damaged by the continuing effects of the German Luftwaffe's aerial assaults on the capital. The situation was deteriorating resulting in the loan of nearly 400 buses from across the country. Dundee Corporation in common with other

Scottish operators including Aberdeen, Edinburgh and Glasgow supplied five double deck Leyland TD1s. They were part of a batch of twelve, new in 1931, numbered 35 to 46 (TS 9117-9128). Seating 48 passengers (although they were originally registered as 51 seats) they had been part of an order by Dundee Corporation that would allow them to replace time served trams of the Dundee, Broughty Ferry & District Traction Company in 1931. The twelve were the city's first double deck buses. The buses selected for duty in London were numbered 35, 36, 38, 40 and 44. They served London from the 26th October 1940 until 25th May 1941 when they were returned to their native city - thankfully in one piece. Each bus received a small plaque fixed to the bulkhead in the lower deck to commemorate their service. The majority of the buses would continue to serve Dundee until January 1947 with the final ones being withdrawn in 1948. Little did we know then that this would be the start of an enduring relationship that would still be going strong some eighty years later?

The first of many

Dundee Corporation Transport Fleet Number	Registration Number	London Transport Fleet Number
170	HGC 217	STL2684
171	HGC 218	STL2685
172	HGC 220	STL2687
173	HGC 221	STL2688
174	HGC 223	STL2690
175	HGC 224	STL2691
176	HGC 226	STL2693
177	HGC 229	STL2696
178	HGC 231	STL2698
179	HGC 232	STL2699

Recently arrived from London are five STLs (HGC 223, 231, 217, 220, 218) complete with their London destination blinds still intact when photographed at the foot of Market Street in 1955.

Balunie Avenue is the setting for this view of 170 (HGC 217) in 1957 with not a car in sight.

In 1946 London Transport received twenty AEC Regent IIs STLs (Short Type Lengthened) with the provincial style bodywork by Weymann. Times were changing in postwar Britain and by 1955, as part of a standardisation programme, London Transport deemed these buses surplus to requirements and promptly sold the complete batch to Birds of Stratford Upon Avon who were the largest breaker of buses in the UK in addition to being a dealer at that time. Ten of these buses found their way to Dundee who fitted them with pre-selector gearboxes prior to entering service. 170 was the first on the road on the 1st December 1955 with the remainder joining throughout January with 176 and 179 finally completing the ten on the 1st March 1956.

Dundee bought ten Daimler CVD6s with Weymann bodies similar to the STLs that arrived from London. Native Daimler 75 (CTS 634) sits to the right of ex- London 170 (HGC 217) at King William IV Dock.

With an unidentified tram hot on its heels 173 (HGC 221) heads to Balgay Road on a duplicate duty. The bus was new in February 1946.

Making its way up Victoria Road 170 (HGC 217) is on its way to Douglas with a Thames Trader coal truck belonging to Taylor Brothers to the rear.

Heading up Whitehall Street passing Largs electrical and TV shop is 176 (HGC 226) about to run on service 20 as a duplicate. Largs holds fond memories for many Dundonians of a certain age. It was well known for its basement with guitars hanging on the walls. You could also pick up sheet music and records not to mention electrical appliances making it a must for any budding musicians and the public in the city.

Advertising Dundee's well-known department store DM Browns that had been established in 1888 is 177 (HGC 229) as it turns into Shore Terrace in this late 50s image.

Having a rest outside Maryfield garage is numerically the last Dundee STL 179 (HGC 232) in late October 1964. The bus would be withdrawn from service two months later.

They fitted in well with the Corporation having already bought ten Daimler CVD6s with Weymann bodies in 1953 numbered 70-79 (CTS 629 etc). Serving a variety of routes they ran in Dundee until December 1964 when all ten were sold to a dealer in Salsburgh. Seven were immediately scrapped with the remaining three (173, 177, 179) soldiering on until 1967 before making their way to the breaker's yard. The significance of their withdrawal date was that it heralded the introduction of twenty new Daimler Fleetlines, the first rear engine, front entrance buses for Dundee.

Replacing the trams

Dundee Corporation Transport Fleet Number	Registration Number	London Transport Fleet Number
211	JXC 222	RT1459
212	JXC 178	RT1415
213	JXC 223	RT1460
214	JXC 217	RT1454
215	KGK722	RT1463
216	JXC 218	RT1455
217	KGK 728	RT1469
218	JXC 173	RT1410
219	KGK 732	RT1473
220	JXC 175	RT1412
221	KGK 733	RT1474
222	JXC 182	RT1419
223	KGK 735	RT1476
224	JXC 184	RT1421
225	KGK 742	RT1483
226	JXC 185	RT1422
227	KGK 744	RT1485
228	JXC 186	RT1423
229	KGK 752	RT1493
230	JXC 187	RT1424
231	KGK 761	RT1502
232	JXC 191	RT1428
233	KGK 762	RT1503
234	JXC 196	RT1433
235	KGK 766	RT1507
236	JXC 197	RT1434
237	KGK 774	RT1515
238	JXC 198	RT1435
239	KGK 780	RT1521
240	KGK730	RT1471

The RT had been in production since 1939 but only went into mass production after the Second World War ended. The design, with a lower mounted engine and very low bonnet line, gave unrivalled visibility to the driver. With their functionality, advanced styling, bright interiors and comfortable seating they were arguably ahead of their time. These handsome buses used standardised interchangeable parts to drive down repair times and costs. Made famous in the 1963 Cliff Richard British classic film 'Summer Holiday' it was familiar to many although ultimately eclipsed by its successor the Routemaster despite the fact that 5000 more RTs were produced. The Routemaster would also see service in Dundee but more of that later. Bodybuilders, Park Royal and Weymann built the majority but shortages of labour and materials meant that to speed up production non-standard body builders would have to be used. This introduced non-standard body builders Cravens and Saunders buses to the streets of London. Although production ceased in 1954 the type actually served London for forty years with over 7000 examples being produced. Our interest in Dundee is around the bodies built by Cravens Railway Carriage and & Wagon Company of Sheffield. The company built 120 RTs distinguished by their five bay window design as opposed to the four bay, noticeably different front and rear curvature compared to the standard RT. Their bespoke mountings meant that their bodies were not interchangeable with the standard RT chassis meaning that they could not be mixed with standard bodies during overhauls. 93 received the standard red and cream livery familiar to those in the capital with the remaining 27 receiving London Country's green and cream livery and were allocated to Watford High Street or Windsor garages. However as with the previously mentioned AEC Regent STLs, London Transport in the mid 1950s began to standardize its bus fleet. Bus use had decreased dramatically at that time and London Transport had more buses than it was ever going to need meaning that the non-standard RTs became surplus to requirement. These buses were relatively young and maintained to a high exacting standard with the majority being just seven years old making them an ideal purchase. Once again the buses were sold to Birds of Stratford Upon Avon who offered thirty to Dundee Corporation as part of a deal to scrap the trams and their infrastructure. As has been discussed in my book 'Dundee Buses – Green to Blue', Dundee Corporation Transport snapped up thirty, which allowed them to speed up the withdrawal of the tramway network in the city.

Sitting in the yard at the foot of Market Street are RTs JXC196, 186 & 184 (soon to be 234, 228 & 224) having arrived from London and awaiting preparation before entering service in Dundee. One of the first things to be removed will be the front fog lamp deemed to be an unnecessary extravagance on the Corporation's buses.

The lower deck interior of an unidentified Dundee RT shows the rope bell running along the roof of the bus. It still has a London Transport information notice on the driver's window.

The services to Fintry were numbered 31-34 with the latter being an infrequent peak time service. Spending time on the 31 is 213 (JXC 223) prior to receiving the simplified livery as worn by 238 (JXC 198) just to the rear in this High Street view in 1963.

The trams were now a fading memory as 235 (KGK 766) sits on the cobbles in Perth Road in 1957.

Here we have a rear view of 230 (JXC 187) showing the route number blind, which still has the framework of the old London arrangement. On its next repaint it would be panelled over with just the route number blind showing.

The RT's were garaged at Maryfield and were used almost exclusively on the Fintry services although the odd stray did appear elsewhere if operational necessity dictated it. They took to the road on Sunday 21st October 1956, the first day after the last tram had run in service. The buses retained their front route number roof boxes making them unique in Dundee and easily recognisable even from a distance. The comprehensive front London style destination and intermediate points blind were not retained; instead they were altered to give them a rather limiting one aperture above the lower deck. The side and rear route number apertures were also amended to have a small aperture. The side aperture would be panelled over after their first repaint together with the rear being altered to fit only a route number. Another feature was the rope bell that stretched from one end of the saloon to the other and, like the STLs, had windows that could be wound up and down to improve ventilation, a feature not previously seen in Dundee. The buses served Dundee well; they had been new in 1949/ 50 and would last until 1969. Many lamented their withdrawal as both crews and passengers universally liked them; although they were a little skeptical to begin with, all were sorry to see them go off to that big scrapyard in the sky. Four managed to escape and went on to work in different guises with 233, 235 going to Dundee Corporation Building Department. The former had its body removed and received an old lorry flatbed which was attached to its chassis to allow its further use. 237 and 239 were reported as being used as staff caravans by Stephen (Builders) of Perth until the late 1970s

Albert Square is the setting for 231 (KGK 761) on its way to Windsor Street on service 36. The service to Windsor Street at peak time was every thirty minutes.

Stopped in traffic in Meadowside 239 (KGK 780) should be on its way to Fintry on the 32. Its driver looks to be exiting the bus as the driver of the Brush-bodied Daimler CVD6 17 (BTS 497) behind looks to negotiate his way around the stricken vehicle.

The terminus for service 36 was at Magdalen Yard Road at the foot of Windsor Street with the Tay Rail Bridge and the River Tay in the background making it arguably the most scenic in the city. Waiting to return to Fintry is 236 (JXC 197).

Having received a repaint of all-over green with a simple narrow white band 211 (JXC 211) is going nowhere quickly as it sits on the forecourt at Maryfield garage minus its engine.

St Andrew Street provides the setting for Dundee Corporation RT 219 (KGK 732) as it heads into the city centre.

Dundee's Buses — *London Calling*

Having arrived at Albert Square 212 (JXC 178) pauses before heading off to the Sinderins. The bus is advertising BOAC (British Overseas Airways Corporation) that in 1974 merged with BEA (British European Airways) to form what we know today as British Airways PLC.

Featured for a second time 220 (JXC 175) sets of from the traffic lights in the Dundee High Street. To the left of the bus is the rear of a new Daimler Fleetline on service 20 to Downfield.

A lovely summer's day sees 220 (JXC 175) heading for Windsor Street on service 36. This bus had been the first bus to run to Ninewells the day after the tram service ceased.

238 (JXC 198) does a turn on service 33 to Fintry in this late Fifties view. The bus had been new to London Transport in May 1949 and was one of the last to be withdrawn by Dundee in 1969.

The High Street looking west before the Overgate was developed shows 228 (JXC 186) in this period picture. A Daimler CVG6 likely 200 (ETS 980) is just behind on service 20 to Downfield.

The drivers of 221 (KGK 733) and 228 (JXC 186) appear to be having a bit of banter as the traffic lights in the High Street change to green. The relatively new Daimler Fleetline 52 (CYJ 853D) completes the line-up as it loads for Menzieshill in 1967.

In October 1965 228 (JXC 186) passes through the High Street on its way to the Sinderins. At peak times the headway from the High Street was every two minutes.

Away from its usual hunting ground of the Fintry services 233 (KGK 762) looks to have completed a journey on the circular service 7 as it sits unattended in Dock Street.

On football match duty is 234 (JXC 196). The bus was unique in that it had its London style vertical opening side windows replaced by standard DCT types. These windows look to have been donated from a withdrawn bus although its identity is unknown. In my opinion it looks an unhappy fit and does little to enhance the bus's appearance.

Having returned to Shore Terrace 238 (JXC 198) waits for its next duty on the 16th June 1964. The 1A service would normally have been the preserve of a Marchbanks based bus so given that Maryfield was the home depot of 238 we can only assume that the bus was filling in due to a vehicle shortage .

Heading along the Nethergate is 239 (KGK 780) with a 1965 Mercedes following behind. The view along the High Street would soon see a dramatic change as all the buildings to the rear of the bus would soon be demolished to make way for the 'new' Overgate.

Advertising McVitie's digestive biscuits is 240 (KGK 730) numerically the last of Dundee's RTs. Despite the name these biscuits don't actually help with digestion but are still a big seller today with 4.4 million consumed daily.

Having completed thirteen years in Dundee 239 (KGK 780) was finally withdrawn and bought by Stephen a building contractor in Perth to act as a staff canteen and rest room.

Here we have three withdrawn Dundee Corporation buses (56 YJ 9129, 125 AYJ 377 and 235 KGK 766) now painted light grey sitting in the Dundee Corporation Building Department HQ in Clepington Road Dundee on the 24th March 1972.

With the bus body now removed the chassis of ex 233 (KGK 762) has a flatbed attached to it so it can be used as a lorry by the Building Department.

Capital adventures

Daimler Fleetline 305 (GYJ 405G) was purchased new by Dundee Corporation Transport and entered service in March 1969. Initially to be used on the St Mary's routes (1, 1A, 1B, 2) it would migrate to other routes usually worked from the Marchbanks depot where it was based. It had been part of a batch of ten 296-305 (GYJ 396-405G) that had an Alexander 'J' type body. Numerically 305 was the last 'J' type to enter service with Dundee Corporation Transport. Sadly the bus suffered a serious arson attack in July 1973 putting it out of service for nearly two years languishing at the back of East Dock Street depot covered by a tarpaulin before being repaired and restored to regular bus duties. Upon its withdrawal from service in 1980 the in-house team converted it to an open top bus painted white with a dark blue band between the decks.

The initial conversion had no small side windows in the upper deck which gave the bus a slightly top heavy look. This however was remedied and the result was a conversion, which was sympathetic to the original look of the vehicle.

It was renumbered 301 for its latter years in service but in truth, apart from the summer months where it could be found on almost any regular route and on the Dundee holiday fortnight service to Broughty Ferry, it was rarely seen. By 1985 it was sold to the London Tour Company for sightseeing tours around the capital. Painted in an attractive red with a gold band it certainly did not look out of place on London's streets. It was last noted as being owned by Ensign of Purfleet and it was reportedly exported although its whereabouts are unknown.

Sitting in the High Street is the recently converted 305 (GYJ 405G) without any side windows in the upper deck. The bus has arrived in the city centre from Broughty Ferry on service 66 which usually ran during the Dundee summer holiday fortnight.

Renumbered 301 (GYJ 405G) to make way for the arrival of the Plaxton-bodied Leyland Leopard coaches in early 1982, the bus sits in East Dock Street depot with the upper deck windows fitted giving the bus a more pleasing look in my opinion.

Dundee's first open top bus (GYJ 405G) found its true purpose in London performing sightseeing duties in the capital.

Off to new pastures

Tayside Fleet Number	Registration Number	Boro'line Fleet Number
111	LES 48P	911
113	NSP 313R	912
114	NSP 314R	913
115	NSP 315R	914
116	NSP 316R	915
118	NSP 318R	916
119	NSP 319R	917
122	NSP 322R	918

Boro'line Maidstone formerly Maidstone Borough Council Transport was the municipal bus operator of Maidstone the largest town in Kent and the surrounding area. Given that the theme of the book is London buses you may feel that the inclusion of Boro'line is stretching a point. However the Transport Act 1985 meant that the Council divested its bus services into an arms length company and became trading as Boro'line with an attractive yellow, blue and grey colour scheme. In the late 80s as with other operators Boro'line looked to expand its area of operation. In January 1988 Boro'line became an early participant in the London Transport route-tendering scheme hence the inclusion in this book.

Looking a bit unloved in East Dock Street depot are Volvo Ailsas 113, 114 and 112 (NSP 313R etc) in early March 1986 as they await their fate following their premature withdrawal.

In June 1988 Tayside withdrew a number of their early Volvo Ailsas leaving them redundant in East Dock Street depot for a few months. Ensign a dealer in Purfleet took fourteen of them with eight finding their way to Boro'line in November of that year for use in the Bexleyheath area on London Regional Transport contracts. They would remain with Boro'line until mid 1992 when the majority were sold to Black Prince of Morley. Tayside developed a good relationship with Boro'line and it was not uncommon to see one of the Ailsas back up in Dundee for mechanical work.

Ex-122 (NSP 322R) now Boro'line Maidstone 918 is parked next to an Optare bodied Leyland Olympian 757 (E157 OMD) at Bexleyheath on the 1st December 1989.

Also at Bexleyheath is ex-116 (NSP 316R) now numbered 915 when seen on the 30th December 1989. The bus originally entered service in Dundee in August 1976.

Now numbered 912 with Boro'line Maidstone ex-113 (NSP 313R) is about to load for its trip to Eltham Station.

Riverside Drive is the setting for this view of ex-119 (NSP 319R) now Maidstone Boro'line 317 when spotted on a test run with a couple of mechanics.

In 1991 after Tayside Regional Council sold its bus operation to its employees I think it would be fair to say that the new company struggled to invest in new buses to lower the average age of the fleet. From the company taking over until sold in 1997 they purchased eighteen buses all single-deck. In February 1997 employee owned Tayside Public Transport Company Ltd (TPTC) was sold to the National Express Group (NEG) and was immediately rebranded as Travel Dundee. Given the age profile of the fleet investment in new buses was needed. The spending power of the Group who were operating hundreds of buses in the West Midlands and London began to show immediately. Brand new buses began to arrive and in the intervening years Dundee's buses were transformed with a combination of new and second hand stock cascaded from other parts of the Group finding their way up to their most northerly outpost. Eleven years later in October 2008 a rebranding took place with National Express Dundee (NED) being the new name on the city streets. The bus livery was changed to red and white. It should be noted that all Travel Dundee's buses gained a '7' prefix to their fleet numbers in the mid 2000s. In 2004 National Express Group entered the London bus market acquiring Travel London that had been part of the old Connex bus operation. They expanded further in 2005 when they purchased the London bus division of Tellings Golden Miller. This proved to be significant in terms of the transfer of ex-London buses north as the Group strived to have a completely low floor fleet in Dundee. Tayside had operated the UK's first low floor bus, a Scania N113 with an East Lancs MaxCi body in 1993 numbered 114 (L3 LOW). It also operated Scotland's first low floor double deck bus. Fleet number 2 (R2 NEG) was a DAF DB250 with an Optare Spectra. Without question NEG's investment in Dundee transformed what had been an ageing fleet into a modern one with the average age reduced significantly. Unsurprisingly given their track record in innovation Travel Dundee became the first to operate a 100% low floor large fleet in the UK – quite an achievement. The reason for giving this background is that the desire to maintain their low floor aspirations meant that buses could be transferred from other parts of the NEG Empire hence the introduction of the Optare Solos and Optare Excels all of which had served time in London. That said there were five non-low floor buses that initially joined the Tayside Greyhound coaching arm. These Volvo Olympians having previously served airport routes in and out of London were fitted with coach seats and were felt to be a good fit for Greyhound's private hire and school contract fleet.

Travelling in style

Travel Dundee/ NED Fleet Number	Registration/ Re-Registration Number	Comments
269	R91 GTM, USU 661	Note 1
270	R92 GTM, USU 662	Note 1
271	N128 YRW, VSR 591	Note 2
272	N125 YRW	Note 3
273	N126 YRW	Note 4

Note 1: Transferred to Dundee August/September 2005. Originally numbered TC25 & 26 respectively.

Note 2: Transferred to Dundee December 2006. Numbered 3128 with Travel West Midlands.

Note 3: Transferred to Dundee December 2006, then to Wolverhampton December 2006 returning to Dundee February 2008. Numbered 3125 with Travel West Midlands.

Note 4: Transferred to Dundee February 2008. Numbered 3126 with Travel West Midlands.

N125 YRW new to London United (Airbus) in May 1996 is seen here in Victoria sponsored by Toshiba prior to it becoming Travel Dundee 7272. (Mark Bowerbank)

Originally numbered TC26 (USU 662) soon to be 7270 is pictured in the purple livery of Tayside Greyhound when spotted at Camperdown Leisure Park.

Double deck Volvo Olympians 269 and 270 had Northern Counties Palatine II bodies. Seating 68 passengers and fitted with coach style seats they had originally been purchased by Cambridge Coach Services then passed to National Express Airlinks. Their arrival in Dundee saw them painted in the rather uninspiring all over purple Travel Greyhound livery, the coaching arm of Travel Dundee numbered TC25 and TC26.

Ultimately they would move to the bus fleet when Travel Greyhound became consigned to the history books with the buses painted into National Express Dundee's red and white before they were both sold in May 2013. 271-273 were also long wheelbase Volvo Olympians this time with arguably the more attractive Alexander Royale bodywork. Purchased in 1996 by London United (not a football team but one of twelve operating subsidiaries of London Buses that commenced operation on the 1st April 1989) they were to be used on the Airbus services A1 and A2 that were originally sponsored by Toshiba that connected Heathrow Airport with central London. National Express purchased the Airbus business of London United in 2000. After a few years with different operators they found their way to National Express West Midlands before ending up in Dundee. Originally the buses were fitted with 52 seats, 43 upstairs and only 9 downstairs and had air conditioning. However 271 was reseated to 64 and 272/273 reseated to 60 and could typically be found on school and shopper bus services'

After losing the Tayside Greyhound livery 7269 (USU 661) looks a bit more businesslike in the National Express Dundee (NED) livery when photographed on school duties as it waits for pupils from Dundee High School.

These stylish buses were used on the Dundee High School contracts which could see the buses travelling as far as St Andrews, Bridge of Earn, Forfar and Blairgowrie. Initially they also ferried pupils to and from Arbroath but this soon passed to Travel Wishart given their proximity to the Angus town. At times, vehicle shortages in the bus fleet led to all the Olympians being used in semi-regular service despite having a step entrance. 271 arrived in Travel Greyhound's purple livery and subsequently gained the red and white of National Express Dundee, the only one of the three to be treated in this way with 272 and 273 in Travel Dundee livery. All would leave Dundee in May 2013.

Crossing the High Street, Murraygate and Commercial Street junction 7269 (USU 661) is heading for the Dock Street depot in this 2012 view.

Usually worked by smaller buses 7270 (USU 662) has returned in one piece from the rural tendered service 139 which served the narrow country roads around Auchterhouse and Tealing.

Although the NED fleet was claimed to be 100% low-floor 7271 (VSR 591) is pictured on the 22 to Craigowl but by no stretch of the imagination could it be described as 'buggy friendly' not to mention the majority of its seats were upstairs.

The lack of a lower rear window in favour of the air conditioning unit is evident in this view of 7271 (VSR 591).

Another journey for 7271 (VSR 591) is the X39 to Carnoustie that was a tendered service that ran infrequently and so it was lucky to get this peak morning view in November 2012. The X39 would change at Carnoustie to an 81 to Forfar then at Forfar to a 27 to Friockheim.

Time to Excel

Travel Dundee Fleet Number	Registration Number	Travel London Fleet Number
202	R410 HWU	410
203	R404 HWU	404
204	R402 HWU	402
205	R408 HWU	408
206	R403 HWU	403
207	R405 HWU	405
208	R409 HWU	409
209	R990 EWU	TGM 990
210	R992 EWU	TGM 992
211	R991 EWU	TGM 991
212	R985 EWU	TGM 985

In July 2003 Travel London sent seven low floor Optare Excel L960s north for service in Dundee. Prior to entering service sister company Travel West Midlands converted them to a single door layout at their Walsall facility. Numbered 202-208 they seated 34 passengers. The buses were quickly pressed into service with many still waiting to have their route number blinds fitted. Their introduction allowed the step entrance Dennis Darts (30-35 J997 UAC, J853 TRW, J348 GKH, K918-916 FVC) (108-109 K 408/9 MSL) to be withdrawn to help the company achieve its aim of a complete low floor fleet. These stylish small buses were used predominantly on the less patronised services such as the 2, 7, 8, 36, 37 and 55. They would last five years in Dundee before being transferred back south to Birmingham for further service before being withdrawn in 2011.

Seen whilst working for Travel London is (R409 HWU) on route C1. As you will see the bus when new has a centre exit. The bus gained the fleet number 208 once it migrated north to Dundee. (Ed Dales)

202 (R410 HWU) is minus the route number blind and relies on a paper number attached to the windscreen as it performs a duty on service 55 in this view from October 2002 in Laird Street.

The western side of the circular 7 service had changed considerably over the previous forty or so years. By 2002 the route now served Rankine Street, Kilberry Street and Albany Terrace where 203 (R404 HWU) was caught on camera.

Interestingly when the front destination blinds were fitted the positions were reversed with the route number on the left hand side and the destination on the right as seen here on 203 (R404 HWU).

Summer 2005 sees two of Travel Dundee's mid-sized buses in Albert Square that had originated from south of the border. Ex-Travel London 206 (R403 HWU) sits alongside a Wright Crusader Volvo 60 (P522 EJW) that had previously operated for Travel West Midlands in Birmingham as 522.

Put to work almost as soon as it arrived 207 (R405 HWU) waits for passengers minus a destination screen and using only a paper route number placed in the windscreen.

Travel Dundee's 208 (R409 HWU) appears to be heading for Forfar if you believe the destination blind. The bus should have been showing 'Circular' as it heads up Caird Avenue.

The number 7 prefixes the fleet number as seen here in this view of ex-206 now 7206 (R403 HWU) in Union Street.

In October 2006 to supplement the original seven an additional four 35 seat Optare Excels headed north, this time as L1000s that had been originally owned by Tellings Golden Miller. Once again prepared for service by colleagues in Birmingham 209 and 212 wore the standard Travel Dundee livery whilst 210 and 211 were painted in the silver and blue 'Ferry Link' livery. The 'Ferry link' services 9X and 10X operated four buses per hour between Barnhill, Broughty Ferry, city centre and Perth Road to Ninewells Hospital. The two specially prepared joined five other Wright-bodied Volvo single deck buses (147, 148, 162-164 R147 RSN etc) to operate the route although the Excels did stray occasionally on to the network when necessary. The four Excel L1000s, 209-212 were withdrawn and sold locally between April and October 2009 having barely completed three years service in Dundee.

Pictured when service buses used to go into the Camperdown Leisure Park 209 (R990 EWU) is a recent addition to the Travel Dundee fleet.

Pictured in the attractive blue and silver 'Ferry Link' livery 7210 (R991 EWU) sits in Whitehall Street. On closer inspection you will note that the destination blind is showing Barnwell mistakenly instead of Barnhill... oops.

Fitted with electronic route and destination blinds 7211 (R992 EWU) is off its usual route as it deputises on service 7.

Crossing the car park, which has been used as a temporary roadway due to road works in Dock Street, is 7211 (R992 EWU) on a Sunday morning service to Kirkton.

Unusually prior to being sold 7211 (R992 EMW) had its electronic destination screens replaced with the more conventional Day-Glo blinds.

Going Solo

Travel Dundee/ NED Fleet Number	Registration Number	Travel London/ Connex Fleet Number
0321	YT51 EBC	245
0322	YT51 EBD	246
3236	S236 EWU	236
3237	S237 EWU	237
7241	S233 EWU	233
7242	S231 EWU	231
7243	S235 EWU	235
7344	YP02 LCA	S249
7345	YP02 LCE	S251

Passing beneath the walkway connecting Tayside House to the Podium block at the foot of Crichton Street is 321 (YT51 EBC) whilst on service 23 to Woodside. This bus had seen service in Coventry prior to its move to Dundee.

As early as 2002 Optare Solo M850s began to appear in Dundee. The first to arrive were two from Travel West Midlands numbered 200-201 (T304/ 282 UOX) followed by a number of Birmingham cast-offs between 2009 and 2013. From 2006 additional small capacity buses that had served in London began appearing periodically. I have to declare at the outset that these were perhaps my least favourite buses that have performed their duties in Dundee over the years. That said I realise that they performed a useful service particularly on routes where patronage was poor, low floor was needed or it was unsuitable for larger buses. The buses had arrived in the city having previously worked for Connex Bus UK and then after they sold the business to National Express Group who rebranded as Travel London. They also spent some time with Travel West Midlands in Birmingham and/ or Coventry prior to their journey north. Seating between 26 to 28 passengers, some of the 'S' registrations had originally been used on the C1 route for Travel London serving Victoria, Sloane Square, Knightsbridge, South Kensington through to Earls Court and Kensington High Street. Many Dundonians sitting on one of these small buses would have had no idea about the 'posh' postcodes that their bus would have previously served. Originally a number were transferred to G&N Wishart based at Friockheim, a village some 20 miles northeast of Dundee, which had been taken into the National Express Group as part of the National Express Dundee's rural and coach arm. Wishart's operated as a separate entity with a mix of service, contract and private hire work. The Solos served some tendered services in the Arbroath area. However, all of these buses performed service work in the city when they were transferred north between 2006 and 2012. After that date more West Midlands Solos would arrive taking the total to 22 of that type to operate in Dundee between 2002 and 2013. There is little doubt that National Express Group's investment transformed the fleet coupled with Dundee City Council's successful bid for £12 million funding from the Scottish government for the Smartbus Project. The project was to improve the overall public transport offering in the city through on-street infrastructure, real-time information, CCTV in buses and an overall improvement in the transport information being provided to the general public.

322 (YT51 YTB) stops in Union Street with the mast of the RSS Discovery in the background on the little used service 43.

Dundee's Buses — London Calling

Camperdown Leisure Park is the setting for these views of Optare Solo 3236 (S236 EWU) in the summer sunshine of 2002.

New in December 1998 to Travel London 7241 (S233 EWU) is in Travel Dundee livery heading east along Dock Street.

Now freshly painted in National Express Dundee livery is 7242 (S231 EWU) although the number 7 is missing from the beginning of the fleet number in June 2012.

Having previously spent time with Travel Wishart 7344 (YP02 LCA) is seen in Commercial Street having been transferred to Travel Dundee. The bus is on the tendered service 208 to Claverhouse in October 2011.

Repainted into NED livery 7345 (YP02 LCE) returns from the tendered country service 139 as it heads down King Street in the summer of 2012.

Refreshing the fleet

Xplore Dundee Fleet Number	Registration Number	London United Fleet Number
8961	YX62 BPU	ADE40468
8962	YX62 BCK	ADE40448
8963	YX62 BPO	ADE40467
8964	YX62 BKF	ADE40459
8965	YX62 BPZ	ADE40469
8973	YX62 BCV	ADE40449
8974	YX62 BGE	ADE40452
8975	YX62 BJZ	ADE40458
8976	YX62 BLZ	ADE40461
8977	YX62 BPF	ADE40466
8978	YX62 BBZ	ADE40447
8979	YX62 BNV	ADE40465
8980	YX62 BGF	ADE40453

On the 1st January 2021 McGill's Buses purchased Xplore Dundee from National Express Group in a surprise deal. In 2023 the McGill Group took the opportunity to purchase twenty RATP London United (on loan to Abellio) AD Enviro 400s with dual doors. The buses were split between the Group's companies - Midland Bluebird, Eastern Scottish and Xplore Dundee numbered 8961-8980. Helpfully they were compliant with London's LEZ laws making them ideal for Dundee's soon to be introduced central LEZ. Initially buses 8965, 8973 and 8975-8980 were purchased to convert service 1 St Mary's to double deck operation to accommodate recovering passenger numbers following the Covid pandemic. They were converted to single door, refurbished and repainted into an attractive updated version of the Xplore Dundee livery by Ensign Bus in Purfleet on Thames.

The Stack Leisure Park has changed significantly since its initial inception as 8976 (YX62 BLZ) makes its way to the bus stop.

Courthouse Square is the starting point for 8977 (YX62 BPF) prior to it setting off for St Mary's on service 1.

Pictured at the St Mary's terminus is 8978 (YX62 BBZ) that had been new to London United in October 2012. The swooping lines of the new Xplore Dundee livery suit the bus in my opinion.

8979 (YX62 BNV) makes its way along Pentland Avenue as it runs on service 17 to Whitfield on a sunny afternoon in 2024.

This view shows the different liveries of the AD Enviro 400s that belong to Xplore Dundee. 8980 (YX62 BGF) has the Xplore livery while 8964 (YX62 BKF) has the livery originally applied to the ex-Eastern Scottish that were transferred up to Dundee in late 2023.

When McGill's Scotland East scaled back its Eastern Scottish branded operations on Edinburgh City Council tendered services it freed up the five ex-Eastern Scottish liveried buses 8961-8964 and 8974 from their Livingston depot. Given their recent painting into Eastern Scottish green and cream livery, Xplore Dundee took the decision to retain it and brand them for the 32/33 Fintry/ Whitfield services with the exception of 8964 which has a promotion for individuals to join the Xplore Dundee team.

The contrasts in the rears of ADL 8961(YX62 BPU) and Wright-bodied Gemini 2832 (BU06 CWZ) are evident in this photograph taken in Commercial Street.

A quiet morning in Crichton Street catches 8963 (YX62 BPO) as it shows off the ex-Eastern Scottish livery that has been incorporated for Xplore Dundee's services 32/33.

Prior to receiving advertising to encourage new drivers to join Xplore Dundee 8964 (YX62 BFK) is seen on service 32.

Two of the ex-Eastern Scottish buses retain the orange style electronic destination screen as demonstrated by 8964 (YX62 BPU) the other is 8962.

A sight to see

Season	Xplore Dundee Fleet Number	Registration number	Re-Registration number	London Fleet Number
2022	2850	BF60 UUC	CTS 917	VN37894, VW1846
	2851	BF60 UUE	OTS 271	VN37895, VN1847
	2854	BF60 UUJ	N/A	VW1848
2023	9903	V473 KJN	ACZ 7489	TA99
	9905	X274 NNO	ACZ 7494	TA274
2024	8925	LK08 NVN	N/A	TE897
	8927	LK08 NVP	N/A	TE899

Pausing at the Discover Dundee tour stop outside the RSS Discovery is 9903 (ACZ 7489), which had originally started life with Stagecoach London in November 1999 making the bus 24 years old at this point. (Robert Davidson)

Descending from the Law Hill turning point on the Discover Dundee tour is 8925 (LK08 NVN).

Xplore Dundee launched a Dundee open-top sightseeing tour in early April 2022. Whilst it had been done before by Tayside and then Travel Dundee using the only open top Volvo Ailsa 300 (WTS 272T) this tour actually took passengers across the Tay Road Bridge giving some spectacular views west up the River Tay towards Perth and down towards Broughty Ferry and beyond. Although the tour was subject to the challenges of the Scottish weather it was successful. The initial buses used were a pair of ex Lothian Volvo B9TL Wright Eclipse Gemini 2s numbered 2850 CTS 917 (previously BF60 UUC), 2851 OTS 271 (BF60 UUE) later joined by 2854 (BF60 UUJ). All three had previously been new to First London CentreWest as dual-door buses numbered VN37894-96 then passed to Metroline West as VW1846-8. They were converted to open top for the London City Tour and when that business ended they then went briefly to Julia London City Tours before being acquired by Edinburgh Bus Tours, a Lothian subsidiary, as 251/2/5. The buses' bright red base livery and attractive branding was certainly eye catching although 2854 was unbranded. Interestingly the cherished registration donated to these buses had originally belonged to Tayside with an Irizar Greyhound coach 294 (A946 VGG) and an East Lancs double deck coach 90 (A290 TSN). For the 2023 season a couple of different open-top buses arrived once again with a London background and by now the red had changed to orange but still attractive with amended branding. Numbered 9903 ACZ 7489 and 9905 ACZ 7494 were Alexander ALX 400 Dennis Tridents originally new to Stagecoach London as TA99 (V473 KJN) TA274 (X274 NNO) before being transferred to Stagecoach East at Cambridge. Renumbered as 17099 & 17274 they lost half their roof and centre door for use on the City Sightseeing Tour franchise in that city. In 2019 they joined the First East Scotland fleet numbered 32789 and 32794 that had started a sightseeing tour in Edinburgh under the Bright Bus Tours brand. With McGill's purchasing First East Scotland they migrated further north to Dundee. Bringing things up to date in 2024 another two open top buses arrived. Numbered 8925 LK08 NVN and 8927 LK08 NVP these buses were ADL Dennis Trident Enviro 400s new to Metroline London as TE897/ 899 in 2008 originally dual doored. Their path to Dundee was similar to 9903 and 9905 having been part of Bright Bus. At the time of writing the service is now every sixty minutes so only one bus is used with the other as a spare.

Sitting in Albert Square 8925 (LK08 NVN) poses during a lovely spring day in 2024.

Dundee's Buses — *London Calling*

A&C McLennan- The RT lives on

McLennan Fleet Number	Registration Number	Year withdrawn by McLennan	London Transport Fleet Number
94	JXN 350	1973	RTL27
95	JXN 363	1971	RTL40
85	JXN 370	1973	RTL47
86	JXN 372	1972	RTL49
87	JXN 377	1972	RTL54
None	LUC 72	1972	RTL1065
None	LYF 53	1972	RTL1129
None	LYF 57	1972	RTL1133
None	LYF 60	1972	RTL1136
None	LYF 89	1972	RTL1148
None	LYF 115	1976	RTL1174

For some years after Dundee Corporation's last RTs ran in service it was still possible to see Perthshire operator A&C McLennan's ex-London Transport RTLs carrying out duties on the Dundee-Errol service. The history of the company is worth pausing to look at. Alexander (Sandy) McLennan had started the business on the 1st April 1945 to take over services that had previously been provided by William Armstrong of Spittalfield who traded under the name Spittalfield and District Motor Service since 1923. The company covered Perth to Spittalfield and Spittalfield-Blairgowrie services, the latter having three different variations covering Dunkeld, Clunie & Essendy and Lethendy. Sandy had previously worked for Armstrong as a driver and engineer so knew the territory well. A further acquisition in 1946 saw the business take over the Perth to Stanley and Errol services from Allan and Scott of Stanley. Over the next few years further growth saw the company establish a service between Errol and Dundee. Spittalfield was the main premises for the bus operation with depots also in Perth (opened 1952/53), Blairgowrie (opened 1960), Errol and Stanley. There were no formal depot allocations and buses were sent to depots depending on what was available and required. McLennan first applied to run a Dundee to Errol service in 1947 but this was refused following objections from the Railway Executive and W. Alexander. It would be December 1949 before they were allowed to operate two return journeys on a Sunday with an additional three journeys added in 1950. A Saturday service was introduced in 1953 with a weekdays service following in 1956. The route was Errol, Grange, Inchture Station, Monorgan level crossing, Kingoodie, Invergowrie, and Riverside Drive to Dundee. The Dundee terminus was situated at the east end of Riverside Drive until 1960 when it was replaced with the south stance at Shore Terrace making it a bit more accessible for would-be passengers. When Shore Terrace closed, the terminus was transferred to Yeaman Shore. As was the practice at the time A&C McLennan were prohibited from picking up passengers within the Dundee city boundary on the inward journey and similarly could not drop off on the outward journey.

McLennan's bought a total of eleven ex-London Transport RTLs. The buses had been new to London Transport in the early 1950s and initially five were purchased in 1958 upon their withdrawal from London Transport (February JXN 370, 372, 377 and June JXN 350, 363). A further four would follow in 1963 (LYF 53, 57, 60, 89) with the last two – LUC 72 and LYF 115 arriving in Perthshire from Dunoon Motor Services in February 1965. These Leyland Titan 7RTs had traditional Park Royal bodies as opposed to Dundee Corporation's Craven bodies and seated 56 passengers. The buses were fitted with platform doors at the company's Spittalfield premises. They wore a livery of Oxford blue and a slight off-white making them easily recognisable in the city.

By the early 70s McLennan's fleet had grown to over 60 buses most of which were second hand purchases; however, this would be the peak as services began reducing as car ownership increased rapidly making these rural routes non-viable. The RTLs would be withdrawn between 1971 and 1976.

Here we see a view of the 85 (JXN 370) ready for its return journey to Errol. The fleet number was shown in the same engine cover panel where London Transport would have had theirs.

A rather grainy image of A&C McLennan's ex London Transport RTL 85 (JXN 370) as it arrives at the Riverside Drive terminus of the Errol-Dundee service.

Sandy McLennan died in 1972 and the strength of the fleet quickly dropped before dwindling to 26 by November 1985. McLennan's surrendered the Dundee to Errol licence on the 31st January 1981 with Tayside Regional Council (TRC) taking over the service. The service ran with McLennan vehicles 'on hire' to TRC until a new operator could be found. From the 22nd February 1981 Tay Valley Coaches operated the service on TRC's behalf. The contract would pass to Stagecoach on the 4th March 1985. It was perhaps a bit ironic given where the licence for the service ended up that in November 1985 the company's assets and services were taken over by Stagecoach. As part of the agreement Stagecoach were allowed to use the McLennan name for a limited period. Most of the fleet was withdrawn within the year and so the A&C McLennan name was consigned to the history books.

Strathtay Scottish and its successors

The return of the clippie

Writing a book about London buses in Dundee would be impossible without looking at the iconic London Routemaster's significant contribution in the city. The influence these buses had on the travelling public cannot be under estimated during the late 80s and early 90s.

Strathtay Fleet Number	Registration Number	Re-registration Number	London Transport Fleet Number
SR1	WLT 943	WTS 225A	RM943
SR2	VLT 298	WTS 245A	RM298
SR3	WLT 759	WTS 329A	RM759
SR4	17 CLT	YTS 973A	RM1017
SR5	WLT 702	WTS 404A	RM702
SR6	821 DYE	YSL 32B	RM1821
SR7	691 DYE	WTS 87A	RM1691
SR8	WLT 921	YTS 892A	RM921
SR9	VLT 217	WTS 131A	RM217
SR10	WLT 427	YTS 867A	RM427
SR11	WLT 743	WTS 268A	RM743
SR12	VLT 183	WTS 101A	RM183
SR13	VLT 42	WTS 97A	RM42
SR14	ALD 911B	YSL 76B	RM1911
SR15	ALD 874B	N/A	RM1874
SR16	WLT 610	WTS 316A	RM610
SR17	VLT 93	WTS 109A	RM93
SR18	ALD 914B	YSL 75B	RM1914
SR19	VLT 221	WTS 128A	RM221
SR20	WLT 917	WTS 102A	RM917
SR21	VLT 26	XSL 220A	RM26
SR22	VLT 191	AST 416A	RM191
SR23	VLT 45	AST 415A	RM45
SR24	143 CLT	WTS 186A	RM1143
SR25	WLT 316	WTS 333A	RM316
SR26	WLT 699	WTS 887A	RM699

The Scottish Bus Group formed Strathtay Scottish Omnibuses Ltd in 1985 taking in the southern part of Northern Scottish and the eastern parts of Midland Scottish's operations to ready the company for bus deregulation in October 1986. Strathtay Scottish essentially covered Tayside and was mostly an out of town provider of routes around Dundee to such exotic places as Perth, Blairgowrie, Arbroath, Montrose and Forfar amongst others. They also had trunk routes running through Dundee and a depot in the city hence the connection to this book. The company would be sold to Yorkshire Traction in 1991 and operated as a subsidiary company until 2005 renaming the company Strathtay Buses. Ironically Yorkshire Traction Group was purchased by Stagecoach on the 14th December 2005 for £26 million such were the vagaries of the bus industry. With the onset of deregulation Strathtay's bosses anticipated potential competition from Tayside Public Transport in Dundee and Stagecoach in Perthshire, which could result in the company being squeezed so, clearly, they had to start thinking out of the box. After a successful trial of two Clydeside Scottish Routemasters - RM 219/272 (VLT 219/272) in Perth and Dundee during late 1985 Strathtay Scottish initially bought twenty Routemasters (RM) from London Transport. At circa £4000 per bus they were seen as a cheap way of expanding the fleet and using against any potential threats that deregulation might throw up. If the idea failed the outlay was such that this would likely be recouped with relative ease. With deregulation approaching, Tayside did not register any of the existing joint Tayway services 41, 43, 44 serving Monifieth and Carnoustie that had been in place since 1980. This provided Strathtay with an opportunity to establish some cross-city routes given a lack of buses on the Perth Road corridor. The RM was felt to be a good solution and they would serve on the new deregulated routes 75, 76 and 77 between Carnoustie, Monifieth, Dundee city centre, Ninewells Hospital and Wormit commencing on Monday 27th October 1986. The services would have an average headway of between 6-8 minutes making the RMs ideally suited to this environment. It would re-introduce conductors or 'clippies' after an absence of nine years back on to the city's transport scene. Their presence would speed up the dwell times at bus stops allowing a high frequency service to operate. Prior to this date SR13 (VLT 42) could be seen occasionally performing on the service 41 to Carnoustie.

The buses were collected from Southall London and driven north in convoys. Originally the first nine were allocated to Dundee depot (SR1-SR9) with the remaining eleven working out of Perth depot (SR10-20). These buses were prepared by London Transport in Southall and took to the streets in a striking livery of a predominantly

Pictured in the Seagate depot prior to entering service is SR16 (WLT 610). The bus was new to London Transport in February 1961. (Bob McGillivray)

Another view of the depot at that time shows SR17 (VLT 93) prior to it having its side route number blind fitted. (Bob McGillivray)

The white wheels are certainly shining bright as SR19 (VLT 221) poses at the Seagate bus station prior to entering service. (Bob McGillivray)

blue livery with an orange (marigold) front and diagonal orange and white side stripes with full London style destination blinds. They carried a side route number but the rear destination apertures were not used and were painted over. Initially the wheels were also painted white which in my opinion made them look at bit odd. Bad enough on a new modern bus to have this garish addition but on buses that were by now nearly twenty-six years old, it was a step to far for my taste. These AEC's with Park Royal bodies could seat 64 passengers. Universally liked by both drivers and passengers as a throw back to days gone by, the fact they could be hopped on or off and were staffed by conductors seemed to really catch the public's imagination. The public felt that the presence of conductors was friendly, reassuring, welcoming and ultimately more convenient. In the early days of deregulation, trips to Wormit across the Tay Road Bridge were thought to be the most scenic that could be taken on a Routemaster, subject to weather of course as high sided vehicles and double deck buses are regularly

Service 76 terminated at this stop is in Broomhill Drive Monifieth before looping around the estate. SR1 (WLT 943) has lost its white wheels in favour of a more demure black.

The service to Kingoodie was a challenge for the drivers as it featured a blind sharp left turn over a narrow railway bridge followed by an equally nasty right-hand bend. Happily SR25 (WTS 333A) has just arrived at the Shore Street terminus and will soon set off on the long return journey to Monifieth.

SR2 (WTS 245A), new in April 1960, rests before the return journey east. Although withdrawn in 1992 it went on to see further service in Manchester before being preserved in 1994.

A trip over the Tay Road Bridge is next for SR3 (WLT 759) as it bowls along the High Street. The Wormit terminus sported panoramic views up and down the River Tay, which was almost worth the trip itself.

I am not sure why the bus was parked but here we have SR3 (WLT 759) sitting just off East Dock Street. It was reregistered WTS 329A in August 1988.

Dundee's High Street was a busy through-fare in the 80s as SR2 (VLT 298) follows a Tayside Ailsa heading west. The picture also sees a Fiat Panda and a Ford Capri vying for position amongst the traffic.

Sitting in the High Street is SR6 (821 DYE) whilst on the 76. The bus shelter's advertisements are for the BP share offer helping to date the photograph as October 1987.

SR6 (821 DYE) rumbles along on the 76 when fresh into service with Strathtay. New in February 1964 it lasted until 1992 when it went to the breaker's yard. (Bob McGillivray)

Deregulation of bus services in 1986 allowed Strathtay to service parts of Dundee where their buses had never ventured before. Here we see SR7 (WTS 87A) in Menzieshill heading for Ninewells Hospital.

Negotiating the High Street before it was pedestrianised SR8 (WLT 921) starts the lengthy journey to Monifieth's Ashludie Terrace complete with full London style destination blinds. (Bob McGillivray)

SR8 (WLT 921) is about to be overtaken by a Vauxhall Chevette in this snowy scene in 1986. Production of the Routemaster ceased in early 1968.

SR9 (VLT 217) has just overtaken SR2 (VLT 298) outside the Seagate bus station in this view in late 1986.

Crichton Street is the setting for SR6 (YSL 32B) as it waits for its next run on the 75.

banned from crossing if there are high winds. Ultimately the bridge would prove too much of a problem and the Wormit part of the service was delinked and reverted to one-person operation in early 1987. In March of that year two more RMs were bought (SR21-22) this time with a more traditional livery albeit still using the same blue, orange livery with a white band between the decks. Kelvin Scottish who had also invested in Routemasters were experiencing a chronic shortage of serviceable buses and took these two RMs on loan allocated to their Milngavie depot before they had turned a wheel for Strathtay. SR21 (VLT 26) was fitted with a differential from an RMC (Routemaster coach) and could cruise quite happily at 53mph and was a favourite of the drivers. By mid-summer both buses were allocated to Arbroath depot for use on the 73/74 services between Arbroath/ Carnoustie/ Dundee/ Invergowrie and Ninewells Hospital.

This however only lasted a few months and they were subsequently allocated to Dundee depot as they proved to be unsuitable for that part of the operation. At the time it was the longest RM route in the country covering twenty-four miles end to end. Bigger buses were required for the 73/74 so Strathtay bought second hand Daimler

Strathtay RMs sometimes escaped from the day job. Here SR21 (VLT 26) has stopped off in Carlisle on its way to Showbus at Woburn in Bedfordshire. It is pictured with similar Cumberland Motor Services RM WLT713. Shortly after this as the bus continued on its way down the M6 the bus stopped on the hard shoulder to pick up stranded passengers from a broken down Citylink coach. A happy ending was had as SR21 took all the passengers and their luggage to Blackpool. That's what you call service. (Sholto Thomas)

New in February 1960, SR22 (VLT 191) heads up the hill on Blackness Avenue while on the 74 to Invergowrie. SR22 and 23 spent time on loan to Highland Scottish where they were re-registered AST 415/6A before returning to Dundee in 1989.

The Ashludie turning circle in Monifieth shows SR21 (VLT 26) looking good in the summer sunshine. The bus would eventually be reregistered XSL 220A in April 1990 and numbered 621 prior to its withdrawal in 1994.

Dundee's Buses — *London Calling*

Pictured in Monifieth High Street heading west to Invergowrie is SR22 (VLT 191). When bought by Strathtay the bus spent a couple of months with Kelvin Scottish before turning a wheel for its new owner.

Fleetlines from Manchester to meet the need whilst maintaining conductors on these routes. From August 1987 Strathtay started to re-register their dateless RM registration numbers with the plates finding their way on to a number of the company's coaches and sold to private individuals. In March/April 1988 an additional five RMs were purchased with (SR23-26) prepared for service but sadly RM38 (VLT 38) was deemed to be a non-runner after lying untouched for a few months in Dundee. Strathtay faced severe competition from Stagecoach's Perth Panther operation in 1989 on its Perth city routes. Bus services in Perth had started in 1911 and the Corporation had its own municipal buses until 1934 when their fleet of thirty-five buses was sold to W. Alexander. Buses in the 'Fair City' continued to use the PCT red and cream livery until 1961. As a throwback to Perth City Transport

What would become SR26 (WLT 699) is at the head of the final convoy to leave the old AEC works at Southall on the 13th February 1988. Behind WLT 699 is RM38 and what would become SR23-25. (Sholto Thomas)

Pictured on the 20th May 1989 at Ninewells Hospital on what was thought to be its first day in service with Strathtay is SR26 (WLT 699) that has still to receive a complete set of destination blinds.

Stagecoach tried to compete with Strathtay's RMs for a short time on the Carnoustie-Dundee corridor. Here we see a Leyland National 215 (MAO 369P) new to Cumberland in March 1976. The photograph is dated 29th August 1988. It is on a free service to encourage passengers to defect from Strathtay even going as far as copying the route number. The destination blind is interesting, as I can't recall Stagecoach ever running over the water to Newport at this time.

After being relieved of its duties in Perth following Strathtay's withdrawal from the city SR12 (WTS 101A) is heading for Arbroath minus the route number blind.

By the time this photograph was taken SR12 (WTS 101A) has received a repaint into the more traditional style, which suited the bus.

days and hoping to tap into local support Strathtay responded by painting six of its RMs into the PCT traditional red with a white band between the decks livery. Interestingly the buses chosen were SR1-6, which had all been Dundee based. This resulted in a number of the Perth RMs making their way in the opposite direction for service and ultimately all Strathtay's RMs would spend time working in Dundee. This would not be the last time SR1-6 saw service in Dundee. When the Perth depot withdrew from all their services in 1992 the RMs found themselves transferring back to their old depot. Running in Dundee in full Perth City Transport livery did look a bit odd but

Slightly out of scope but here is ex Dundee RM SR2 (WTS 245A) recently painted into the Perth City livery when pictured in Mill Street Perth.

Venturing up Commercial Street SR3 (WTS 329A) is in full Perth City livery as it works service 51 to Fowlis. This would turn out to be one of the last duties it performed as it passed to preservation not long after the picture was taken. The use of a Routemaster on this service is unusual and was likely caused by a bus shortage with the company stretched covering Citylink duplication given that the picture was taken on Hogmanay. (Sholto Thomas)

Although SR4 (WTS 973A) was now held in reserve it is seen arriving in Dundee from Wormit having crossed the Tay Road Bridge. Its use on this service had been quite deliberate, as road-works en-route in Newport on Tay required a diversion that was not particularly suitable for buses. There was a junction on the diversion that would likely cause damage to the bus rear so SR4 was chosen to be the sacrificial lamb and if you look closely you will see rear end damage. (Sholto Thomas)

The patchwork front of SR23 (AST 415A) is evidence of bits being removed from donor RMs in this view as it leaves Ninewells Hospital on the long return journey to Arbroath. The bus, is best remembered by enthusiasts for being the London Transport radio training bus and as a result it had not seen passenger service for a number of years before joining Strathtay.

SR25 (WTS 333A) could be easily identified, as it was the only Strathtay RM to retain the advertisement frames on either side of the bus, which were fitted by London Transport shortly before its withdrawal.

added to the colour of the city's streets for a time. The daily use of the RMs ended on the 16th August 1993 but SR21 subsequently returned for another six months due to shortages of double deckers, which were required for school and college services. Stagecoach East (Strathtay) continued to operate their Tayway services employing twenty or so conductors using modern, conventional front entrance buses until September 2020 when they announced that due to the increasing use of mobile ticketing and cashless payments together with the on-going effects of the Covid-19 situation they would be withdrawing their conductors. When they ended they were the last provincial service to use conductors and in testament to the job that had been done they lasted twenty-seven years after the last regular Routemasters were withdrawn.

One fact that arose when researching the book, took me a bit by surprise. To celebrate the Queen's Silver Jubilee in June 1977 London Transport painted 25 Routemasters silver with a red relief band and sold off the advertising space on each bus to a single company or advertiser in the February of that year. The bus interiors were refurbished and fitted with a custom made specifically designed wool carpet which featured the London Transport logo, a crown, the dome of St Paul's Cathedral and a Woolmark. Thomson Shepherd Carpets Ltd of

Having been bought by Reading Mainline, 625 following its renumbering from SR25 (WTS 333A) is about to leave Strathtay's now redundant Riggs Road depot in Perth for the long road south complete with Reading trade plates. 624 (WTS 186A) follows just behind (Sholto Thomas)

Dundee made the carpets. As a quirk of fate two of the twenty-five ended up with Strathtay initially at Perth then on to Dundee. The buses were SR14 (ALM 911B) and SR18 (ALM 914B), which is quite a coincidence, and I am not sure what the odds on that would have been in 1977. They were numbered SRM1-25 for the occasion with the two Strathtay examples being SR14 (SRM12 advertising ICL computers) and SR18 (SRM10 advertising Goddard's polish).

This is an interior view of one of the Silver Jubilee Routemasters. The image shows the specially commissioned carpet produced by Thomson Shepherd of Dundee for the occasion (Copyright –TFL from the London Transport Museum Collection).

Having arrived from Monifieth, SR14 (YSL 76B) is heading up the Seagate. Whilst with London Transport the bus had been one of twenty-five selected to be painted silver to celebrate the Queen's Silver Jubilee in 1977.

Making a one-off journey on the 75 was this front entrance RM owned by Clydeside Scottish SMRA1 (KGD 641D). The photograph is interesting for the car park in the background to see how many car makes and models you can identify. This was the only time a front entrance Routemaster ran in service in Dundee. (Sholto Thomas)

In May 1989 a group of enthusiasts made a trip to Dundee on a front entrance RMA that had originally been owned by British and European Airways before being sold to Clydeside Scottish who purchased this and two others although they did not enter service. Clydeside upgraded the bus to a full coach and painted it in their Quicksilver livery. Numbered RMA16 (KGJ 614D) it arrived in Dundee and promptly had a set of destination blinds fitted at the Seagate depot where crews were allocated allowing it to make a round trip to Monifieth. In 2014 Stagecoach East (Strathtay) borrowed one of the Group's heritage fleet RML2444 (JJD 444D) in London red livery to run on service 73 complete with a full 'London' style destination blinds in the lead up to Christmas. The initial plan was for the bus to run alongside the 'new' Routemasters that were to be on loan at that time; alas, this wasn't to be. The next chapter will explain the reasons why. The bus was no stranger to Dundee and made further visits during July 2015 to celebrate Strathtay's 30th anniversary then later in the Decembers of 2015 and 2016.

Part of Stagecoach's heritage fleet RML2444 (JJD 444D) sits in Whitehall Street in December 2014. (Scott Hutchison)

RML2444 (JJD 444D) is on loan to Strathtay during December 2014 when pictured in Monifieth.

Seagate depot is the location for on loan RML 2444 (JJD 444D) parked next to Strathtay's 16932 (WLT 943) an East Lancs Volvo B7TL originally numbered 712 (SP03 GDV). You will note the Volvo's cherished registration plate that had originally belonged to SR1. (Andrew J McIntosh)

Pictured at the Ashludie turning circle in Monifieth on the 23rd December 2016 is a pair of Routemasters. The bus on the left is owned by a local group of enthusiasts. Numbered RML2716 (SMK 716F) it sits alongside Stagecoach East (Strathtay) RML2444 (JJD 444D) although only the one on the right hand side is in service. The significance of the buses displaying 73 is that RML2716 worked this service from 1994 until 2002 in London. This pair entered service eighteen months apart with RML2444 hitting the road in May 1966 followed by RML2716 in November 1967. (Ian Manson)

Of the twenty-six RMs that served Dundee eleven were scrapped when they were withdrawn from service with the remaining fifteen finding homes with new owners in some shape or form. As a testament to the design and the longevity of the type and as if to emphasise the Dundee/ London connection a few of Strathtay's RMs returned to the capital. SR23 (AST 415A) entered service with Sovereign, a subsidiary of RATP Transit London in 2001. The bus was refurbished with a modern interior and had its AEC engine replaced with a Cummings unit. Based at Edgware depot it would give a further four years service before it was finally withdrawn.

A very smart and refurbished, SR23 (AST 415A) looks as if it has never been away as it heads along Oxford Street in the capital. (Sholto Thomas)

SR22 (VLT 191) would also be seen on London's streets but this time as a mobile tearoom for B.Bakery.com. SR2 (VLT 298) has been saved from the scrapyard being fully restored into the original London Transport condition and being reunited with its original registration plate. SR3 (WLT 759) is reported as operational with the London Bus Group. SR26 (WTS 887A) did not stay long in Dundee and was sold to a buyer in Sweden after only six months north of the border after the company was made an offer they couldn't refuse. By my reckoning the two furthest travelled Strathtay RMs are probably SR4 (17 CLT) as a ticket office for Flecha Bus Buenos Aires in Argentina still carrying the registration YTS 973A and SR19 (VLT 221) running open top tours in New Zealand. Given the total number of RMs thought to be in preservation it would be fair to say that they have achieved 'cult' status.

The non-runners

Original Registration Number	Re-Registration Number	London Transport Fleet Number
VLT 38	N/A	RM38
WLT 473	N/A	RM473
WLT 680	N/A	RM680
WLT 784	YTS 565A	RM784
48 CLT	N/A	RM1048
300 CLT	N/A	RM1300

In 1986 London Bus Sales were offering time-served RMs condemned due to their poor "B" frames for £250 each. When you factor in what could be stripped from these buses by way of engines, gearboxes, differentials and body parts it quickly became the most economic way of acquiring spare parts. Six RMs were purchased with this in mind and were broken for spares to help keep the ageing fleet on the road. WLT 680 and 784 were bought and sent to Dundee and Perth respectively and then in mid-1988 48 CLT and 300 CLT replaced them. WLT 473 was also broken for spares in Dundee and Montrose. Originally RM38 was bought at the same time as SR23-26 to be a runner but ended up parked at the rear of Seagate depot and converted to a makeshift boardroom and office space complete with fluorescent strip lights.

Being broken for spares is RM680 that had been new to London Transport in April 1961.

This is the lower deck of RM38's office space whilst sitting in the corner of Dundee's Seagate depot. (Sholto Thomas)

Sitting at the rear of Strathtay's Seagate garage is withdrawn RM38 now being used for spares to help keep the fleet moving.

RM473 is in the process of being broken up for spares. The bus had been new in November 1960 initially allocated to Hanwell depot.

Boris's London legacy

Boris Johnston commissioned the successor to the Routemaster when he was the Conservative London Mayor in 2012. The Routemaster design was by this time nearly fifty-six years old and badly in need of replacement. Various alternatives had been tried most notably the Mercedes Citaro articulated buses which were particularly unpopular and unreliable. Johnston was keen to see a bus that would recreate the appeal of the original Routemaster. In particular he wanted passengers to be able to hop on and off so an open platform at the rear was considered essential. The final design of the bus was controversial to say the least. It had doors at the front, centre and rear. The front and rear doors had staircases, which led to the upper deck. The rear entrance had a platform pole as a nod to the original Routemaster with the door kept open to provide a hop on facility although this was not used during its time in Scotland. Featuring three doors they were certainly a sight to behold when they began service. Seating 62 passengers their capacity was some way short of what was now the accepted normal of between 70 and 83 seats.

This view of the rear of the lower saloon shows the doors complete with middle pole so familiar to many that rode on the old Routemaster.

These upper deck photographs from both angles show the dual staircases at either end of the bus.

The bus was originally known as the New Bus for London then NB4L, the Boris bus, the Borismaster or the official title the New Routemaster. So given Dundee's history with the old RM it was very appropriate that as part of an initiative to evaluate hybrid buses Stagecoach East Scotland (who by now looked after the old Strathtay territory) managed to acquire two new Routemasters in November 2014 which were destined for Stagecoach London. Numbered 61312 (LT312) and 61313 (LT313) and registered LTZ 1312/3 they were built by Wrights of Ballymena. They were to be used as a trial on the service 73 running from Arbroath to Ninewells Hospital via Carnoustie and Monifieth for three months.

A prophetic picture of 61312 (LTZ 1312) over the pits in Arbroath depot prior to entering service.

It was perhaps fitting that Strathtay's original Routemasters had previously served large parts of the route. The introduction of these new buses provided an interesting contrast between the two types. 61313 made its debut outside Wellgate Shopping Centre with specially produced London style destination blinds before Strathtay's own new Volvo B5LH hybrid buses arrived. Sir Brian Souter (who with his sister Dame Anne Gloag had founded Stagecoach Group) was actually the driver of the first 'Borismaster' service on the 73. Unfortunately their time in Scotland was short-lived as they kept breaking down which provided a lot of negative social media and local press coverage at the time with passengers complaining about the poor service. Unfortunately they proved unsuitable for the challenging driving conditions of the Arbroath to Ninewells Hospital service. The reasons for their failure are varied but the route and types of areas being served were very different from those of London. This reduced the buses ability to recharge their batteries as they relied on the engine and regenerative braking to charge them. Across the Tayway 73 route there was far less braking than there would be in central London and the higher speeds particularly in the Carnoustie to Arbroath section, consumed more battery power. This resulted in the battery life being greatly diminished and if the battery dips below a certain charge it effectively becomes dead. It was reported that one of the batteries needed replaced under warranty during its time working the Tayway and the cost was an expensive five-figure sum. The next issue was the interlocks on the open platform at the rear. When the bus stopped to allow passengers to get on or off the bus with the rear platform open, the starting bell had to be pressed from the button on the platform; failing to do this meant the bus could not move leaving the driver powerless and relying on the conductor who could be in another part of the bus taking fares to get to the rear platform pronto. This worked well in London when the conductors were in effect platform attendants but not on the 73's busy cross-city route where the conductor had to collect fares etc around the bus it was a big issue. Their problems proved insurmountable and sadly their time on the 73 was restricted to three weeks instead of the planned three-month trial.

One interesting fact was that both the buses were delivered new to Stagecoach East Scotland rather than Stagecoach London and so became the only two of the type not to go directly to a London operator and the only two to have operated in Scotland.

New bus for London 61313 (LTZ 1313) sits outside the Wellgate Shopping Centre for the launch on the 3rd November 2014. (Andrew J McIntosh)

The rear of 61312 (LTS 1312) shows the three-door design when photographed during its first run into Dundee when unfortunately the 73 in front had to take its passengers due to a mechanical issue.

This was part of the information inside the new Borismaster. Given their performance I am not sure what the passenger reaction would have been.

St Andrew Street is the location for 61312 (LTZ 1312) on its way to Ninewells Hospital on service 73. (Andrew J McIntosh)

Running along the High Street is 61312 (LTZ 1312) on a damp 7th November 2014. The three doors are evident from this view.

The rear platform of 61312 (LTZ 1312) shows the curved glazing off to good effect.

The design of the 'Borismaster' is a bit like Marmite for many; you either love it or hate it?

The Midibus fills the gap

Strathtay Fleet Number	Registration Number	Original Strathtay depot allocation	London Buses Fleet Number
201	J134 HME	Dundee	RB34
202	J235 LLK	Dundee	RB35
206	H129 AML	Dundee	RB29
207	G894 WML	Montrose	RB24
208	G895 WML	Montrose	RB25
209	G892 WML	Dundee	RB22
210	G893 WML	Dundee	RB23

For four years Scottish Bus Group had banned the purchase of new vehicles although Strathtay had been successful in being able to purchase 13 new Renault S56 minibuses to compete against Stagecoach's aggression in Perth in 1989. Following Strathtay's sale to Yorkshire Traction in mid 1991 the company attempted to update its fleet. It is not generally known but the sale prices of the Scottish Bus Group companies heralded by the Government did not include cash in hand which turned out to be quite large sums due to lack of new bus purchases in the preceding years. This cash was also taken by the Scottish Government which was a pity as in Strathtay's case as this amounted to over £2 million, which could have bought around 20 Leyland Olympians at that time. But, as with the other privatised companies, new capital expenditure had to be funded from fares revenue. Yorkshire Traction was under severe competition down south, resulting in Strathtay being effectively on their own with the company 'piggy bank' empty. In any event, subsidies from another area could be deemed to be anti-competitive with severe fines in the deregulated environment. Strathtay resisted the temptation to lease new buses as the situation was so volatile with Stagecoach all around them and Tayside in the middle. In 1991 there was a gap in Strathtay's vehicle parc between 25-seaters and full-size single decks though five Dennis Darts were on order from Wrights that would go to Arbroath depot. The chance to purchase two 'float' Renault S75 midibuses arranged through Yorkshire Traction was very timely. They had been operating on loan to London bus companies as 'warranty spares' and were just two years old. They were J134 HME and J235 LLK numbered 201 and 202 in a new numbering series for such midibuses.

Changed days from when the RMs served Wormit it is now the turn of another ex-London bus 202 (J235 LLK) to head over the river in April 1993. (Sholto Thomas)

On its way into the Seagate bus station with a decent load of passengers is Reeve Burgess bodied 201 (J134 HME). (Sholto Thomas)

210 (G893 WML) was originally allocated to Dundee but it would soon make its way on to the more rural services as seen here near Drumlithie in July 1995. (Sholto Thomas)

At the time the reduced 'minibus' rate of pay agreement at Strathtay was only applicable for up to 25 seat buses so these midibuses and subsequent S75s purchases were considered 'big' buses though this would change around the turn of the century as local wages and conditions evolved. However, the main aim was to replace both elderly, spartan Leyland Leopards and overfull 25 seat minibuses. One of the S75s settled down on the 77B Dundee to Wormit service daytime workings and both generally worked the Dundee city route 36/37 Mill o' Mains tendered evening and Sunday services which required them to be fitted with cash vaults for the exact fare route. For a time one actually had a conductor operated run on the Tayway 8.15am run to Monifieth and return. Yorkshire Traction Group went on to acquire the complete batch of RB Renault 75s from London with a further 5 coming to Strathtay 206-210 (H129 AML, G894/ 95/ 92/ 93 WML) to further modernize the fleet. By this time school contracts were being tendered for and won so they were scattered around the company's depots. They were put to work on Strathtay's country services with their semi-coach seats and they replaced the ageing Leyland Leopards. As is sometimes the case the S75s were only together for scarcely two years under Strathtay's ownership. They were more complicated than the Renault S56 and items could be more difficult to access under the bonnet. They were replaced by a combination of new Dennis Darts and the rebuilt 33 seat MCW Metroriders (211-216). All were passed to Lincolnshire Road Car for further service from 1996 to 2000. It should be noted that missing fleet numbers 203 – 205 (G291/93/92 KWY) were acquired from Harrogate and District in 1993 hence their exclusion from the list.

Going for gold

Strathtay Fleet Number	Registration Number	Comments
10002	SP12 CFU	Note 1
10003	SP12 CFV	Note 1
10004	SP12 CFX	Note 1
10005	SP12 CFY	Note 1
10006	SP12 CFZ	Note 1
10007	SP12 CGE	Note 1
19641	SP60 DSE	Note 2
19642	SP60 DSO	Note 2
19643	SP60 DSU	Note 2
19644	SP60 DSV	Note 3
19645	SP60 DSX	Note 3
19646	SP60 DSY	Note 3
19647	SP60 DSZ	Note 3
19648	SP60 DTF	Note 3
19654	SP60 DPX	Note 4
19655	SP60 DPY	Note 4
19656	SP60 DPZ	Note 4
27547	SP58 BZA	Note 2
27550	SP58 BZD	Note 2
27551	SP58 BZE	Note 5
27552	SP58 BZF	Note 5

Note 1: Allocated to Blairgowrie depot.

Note 2: Allocated to Arbroath depot.

Note 3: Allocated to Arbroath depot and branded for the 73 Tayway service.

Note 4: Allocated to Dundee depot and branded for the 73 Tayway service.

Note 5: Allocated to Dundee depot.

I am sure you will recall the hugely successful Olympic and Paralympics' Games that were held in London in 2012. An event like this requires precision planning and this task was carried out by the LOCOG (London Organising Committee of the Olympic and Paralympics' Games). Transport needed to be provided for the general public, games officials, press and the athletes not just to the Olympic Park at Stratford but also around the rest of London and the across the country. Two of the UK's major bus operators First Group and Stagecoach were engaged to bring the operation together. First Group would have responsibility for buses that the general public would use and Stagecoach would look after the transportation of the athletes, press and officials. Stagecoach Bus Events pooled the Group's resources and organised hundreds of new or nearly new vehicles to come to London from all different parts of the UK. These buses would operate shuttle services. The buses carried small stickers in their front windscreen with rather cryptic destinations such as MMT-MML, MH1-GRP and MM1-ETD. All their advertisements and operator identities were removed. It was reported that the drivers who had been brought to the capital to drive the buses were accommodated in two cruise ships docked on the Thames. One of the headlines of the time highlighted that on the first day some drivers got lost in London bringing athletes from Heathrow Airport to the Olympic Village. However, after that initial glitch services ran very smoothly with at times perhaps over capacity with buses running whether there were passengers on them or not. To contribute to the huge exercise Strathtay sent seventeen of their E40D Enviro double deckers and four Dennis Enviro 300 single deckers to London. These buses were taken from Arbroath, Dundee and Blairgowrie depots. Some of the double deckers were still branded for the Tayway 73 service and the others were buses that predominantly served the 57/59 Perth – Blairgowrie – Dundee services. Their absence was covered by a selection of time served vehicles brought in from different parts of the empire and three new Scania N230UD's from Stagecoach Western. All returned back home once their duties were completed.

Spotted on Olympic Games duty is Blairgowrie based 10006 (SP12 CFZ). Sadly upon its return the bus did not seem to have much luck. It caught fire twice and after the second occasion in January 2023 it never returned to service. (Richard Convey)

Dundee's Buses — *London Calling*

Pictured in Parliament Square London 19655 (SP60 DPY) retains route branding for the 73 but has bits of white tape covering various bits of information regarding things like free wi-fi for example. (Karl Oakley)

Helping to move the crowds during the London 2012 Olympics Games is Strathtay 19656 (SP60 DPZ) that is pictured near Stratford whilst still branded for the Tayway 73 service. (Sholto Thomas)

One of the ADL300 single deck buses 27550 (SP58 BZD) turns right in Russell Square London. MH1-GRP notice in the front window is evident. (Richard Convey)

Perception is reality

Unless you have more than a passing interest in buses the reaction of the public when they see a 'red' bus, is that it is a London bus such is the iconic nature of the red bus and the Routemaster in particular. Over the years there have been a few 'fake' London buses running around the streets of Dundee. In October 1977 a red Dennis Hestair Ltd development bus appeared. It was used on the Fintry/ Sinderins/ Ninewells services, which were still crew operated at that time. This fitted in due the fact that the last half-cabs in service were still being used on the route at that time. The bus, which previously spent time in London, had a Roe body, a Gardner 6LXB engine and a Voith automatic transmission and had been previously owned by Leeds Corporation Transport. London Transport had shown an interest in the bus so it was painted red and ran as a demonstrator on their service 27 between Richmond and Archway. The bus stayed in Dundee for a month before moving on to pastures new. Covered in my book 'Tayside Buses – Blue is the colour', a couple of years later was a preproduction Leyland B15 Titan with a Park Royal body arrived, painted red with the registration number BCK 706R and given fleet number 100 for its stay with Tayside. The bus had a particularly unhappy time in Dundee, more often broken down in the depot, hated by the drivers due to its erratic performance and dubious braking capacity. The bus was almost exclusively used on the 15/17 services Whitfield to Ninewells Hospital. Ultimately, perhaps no surprise given London Transport's own batch of Titan's, the bus found its way to London in 1987 after a period with Fishwicks of Leyland. Not all London buses are red however. An East Lancs Spryte bodied Dennis Dart N251 VPH in London and Country livery appeared in Dundee as part of an attempt to woo Strathtay into buying some buses. East Lancs were part of British Bus and were sold to the Cowie group in 1996 that cancelled all new bus orders at short notice. Such was the crisis at East Lancs that they brought this bus to Dundee for Strathtay to evaluate as they had previously had two Leyland Tiger coaches rebodied and were obviously on the contact list despite the fact that they had been buying buses from Northern Counties and Wrights similar to other Yorkshire Traction Group companies. Strathtay did initially order two longer versions that were numbered 310 and 311 (P310/11 HSN) with a further six following between 1996 and 1999. Yorkshire Traction Group bought buses almost exclusively from East Lancs until 1995.

Painted all over red this Dennis Hestair test bus 7517 UA was to the person in the street a 'London' bus. It spent its time in Dundee on the Fintry/ Sinderins/ Ninewells services and is seen here in Shaftsbury Terrace the terminus for the Sinderins.

Leyland Titan demonstrator 100 (BCK 706R) pictured in East Dock Street depot a place that the bus seemed to spend a lot of its time during its stay in Dundee.

This East Lancs Spryte-bodied Dennis Dart N251 VPH in London and Country livery is pictured here in Dock Street at the rear of the Caird Hall. The bus was not used in service and on its return south it would enter service with London and Country, reregistered as P251 APM and its fleet number was DSL51. (Sholto Thomas)

Although it never ran in service in Dundee, Bankfoot Buses RML2343 (CUV 343C) was photographed at South Marketgait in August 2010. London Transport had a practice of swapping bodies during the overhaul process causing a discrepancy between the chassis and body numbers. DVLA insisted on a physical check being made by one of their employees hence the bus making the visit to Dundee as this was the nearest licensing office. (Graham Martin-Bates)

Postscript

This effectively brings the story of the Dundee/ London connection up to date but after the changes that we have seen in the last eighty or so years it is anyone's guess what the future of the bus exchanges between the two cities will be. I have documented as many of the transfers as I can recall but I am sure there will be the odd one that may have appeared that has slipped through the net so please forgive any omissions.

Reference Materials

Working with Routemasters – Capital Transport

Routemasters around Great Britain – Steve Fennell

Bus Portfolio Routemaster – Geoff Rixon & Steve Fennell

Routemaster Dispersal – Keith A Jenkinson

The London Bus Volume 2 – Celebrating the designs of a British icon

The London Bus Volume 3 – Celebrating a great British icon

London Buses and the Second World War – Ken Glazier

London Transport Buses and Coaches 1939-1945 - John A S Hambley.

With contrasting liveries here we have SR3 and SR25 with their original registrations parked at the Seagate. SR25 (WLT 316) at this point had still to enter service.